JAZZ

JAZZ

HENRI MATISSE

GEORGE BRAZILLER, INC. NEW YORK

Published in the United States of America
by George Braziller, Inc. in 1985.

Jazz by Henri Matisse ©1985 by the Estate of Henri Matisse,
V. A. G. A., New York/S. P. A. D. E. M., Paris.

Introduction ©1983 by Riva Castleman.

Text by Henri Matisse translated from the French by Sophie Hawkes.
English translation ©1983 by George Braziller, Inc.

Library of Congress Cataloging in Publication Data:

Matisse, Henri, 1869-1954.
Jazz.

Originally published: Paris: Editions Verve, 1947.
Bibliography: p.
1. Matisse, Henri, 1869-1954. Jazz. 2. Illustration
of books—20th century—France. I. Title.
NC980.5M35A6613 1983   741.64′092′4   83-11934
ISBN 0-8076-1131-X

CONTENTS

INTRODUCTION

". . . send me a white cane," the dazed Henri Matisse pleaded in March 1944 when he had completed nearly all of *Jazz*'s twenty compositions that he had promised Tériade, the publisher of *Verve*.

During a prolonged convalescence from a serious operation in 1941, Matisse found that one creative activity he could manage while bedridden was to cut painted paper into compositions, a medium he had first used a decade earlier. Yet the penetrating colors of the cut shapes, juxtaposed to form images nothing less than dazzling, were practically driving him blind. Complaining to Tériade that he needed glasses "tinted to 70%," Matisse nevertheless assiduously pursued the application of what was for him a natural tendency to work out an artistic result through the mastery of a relatively mechanical technique.

The brilliant light of the south of France where Matisse now worked demanded the artist respond with overstated colors and intense blacks. These Matisse found in Linel paints which he used to cover the various kinds of drawing papers that were shaped into decorative forms by his agile scissors.

His walls became canvases upon which he composed the cut-out forms, pinned into place by his assistant, Lydia Delectorskaya. Until he considered every area of the composition immutable, the cutting and pinning continued. When the final composition was achieved, the pieces were moved to a less accessible spot on the wall or pasted together and replaced by tentative groupings of more cut pieces. During the years of these cut-paper undertakings, Matisse found it important to see all of his work around him. The colorful papers punctuated the walls, shimmering and fluttering in the breeze like his many pet birds.

The publisher of *Jazz*, Tériade (Efstratios Eleftheriades), was born in Lesbos. He went to Paris to study law in 1915, but soon after worked on the first issues of *Cahiers d'Art*. On his own he proceeded to publish several periodicals before working with another publisher, Albert Skira, on two important illustrated books: the *Metamorphoses* of Ovid, illustrated by Picasso, and the *Poésies de Stéphane Mallarmé*, embellished with etchings by Matisse. It had been Tériade's suggestion that Skira commission Matisse to create the *Poésies*, which turned out to be one of the most beautiful books of this century.

This first successful collaboration seems to have assured a long and creative relationship between Tériade and Matisse. During the early 1930s Tériade directed the destiny of the famous Surrealist-oriented publication *Minotaure*, to which Matisse contributed the cover of the last issue published during Tériade's tenure (No. 9, 1935–36). In 1937 Tériade began his "grande revue artistique et litteraire," *Verve*, with American financial assistance (the title was chosen for its bilingual appeal as the magazine appeared in both French and English). The work of Matisse was featured in most of the early issues, including the first cover which was reproduced from a cut-out composition. Matisse had previously used cut papers to lay out the plan for his mural, *Dance*, for the Barnes Foundation in Pennsylvania (1931–33), and he made his first two complete cut-out compositions in 1936: a maquette for an etching based on the *Dance* mural and a cover for *Cahiers d'Art*. Evidently Tériade encouraged Matisse in this technique and two more cut-outs were made for *Verve*: the first in 1939 for the cover of No. 8, published in 1940; and the second for the cover of No. 13, the summer issue of 1945. The latter cut-out was probably given to Tériade and his assistant, Angèle Lamotte, during their visit to Matisse's studio-rooms in a hotel near Nice in June 1943, when they saw the first two compositions to be used in *Jazz* and a collage of *Icarus*, also used in *Verve*, No. 13. Tériade wrote that it was during this visit that the final plan for *Jazz* was developed, although the original idea for creating a book from cut-outs had been discussed in 1942.

· Most of the collages for *Jazz* relate to some theme from the circus or the theater. An early cut-out, *Rouge et Noir*, that Matisse made in 1937–38 in conjunction with designs for the Ballets Russes de Monte Carlo contains the same tumbling figure that appears in *Toboggan* (plate XX of *Jazz*). The maquette for the 1945 cover of *Verve* included both the tumbling figure and a figure with a flame or star motif similar to that in *The Clown* (plate I). The earliest collages that appear to have been made for *Jazz* were these two, as well as *Pierrot's Funeral* (plate X), *The Nightmare of the White Elephant* (plate IV), and another version of *Icarus* (plate VIII) given by Matisse to Tériade in June 1943. Up to March 1944, by which time he had completed many more of the collages for the book, Matisse had planned to use the title *Circus*. One plate is, in fact, composed with letters spelling out "Cirque" twice, as they would appear on the front and back covers of a book jacket (plate II). Yet, in an interview published in early 1944 he said that the book would be named either *Circus* or *Jazz*.

Since so many plates are devoted to both the classical circus and its music hall equivalent, the change in title has been the subject of considerable conjecture. The decision appears to have been made by 7 March 1944 when Matisse announced in a letter to Tériade that he had completed a collage, "neither Niki Cassecou nor Joseph Cassetout but Plastic Poses" (*Forms*, plate IX), which would replace a circus subject in the book with an abstract one. In the same letter he asked Angèle Lamotte to tell Tériade that he "lacks the paper on which to place my Jazz (or his Jazz)." This is the sole title used in this letter and implies that it was Tériade who began to call the book *Jazz*.

During the Occupation Matisse was burdened not only by poor health but also by the strain of war and concern for the safety of his family. (Mme. Matisse was interned by the Gestapo and their daughter Marguerite was about to be deported.) He was able to continue concentrated work on *Jazz* and other books (*Poèmes de Charles d'Orléans*, Marianna Alcaforado's *Lettres de la religieuse portugaise*, and Baudelaire's *Fleurs du mal*). However, the gay reminiscent subjects of the circus collages gave way to the more abstract figures of *Forms* and *Destiny* (plate XVI), and to the undulating leaf shapes of the three *Lagoon* pictures (plates XVII, XVIII, and XIX).

Three general modes of composition form the basis of Matisse's cut-outs for *Jazz*. There are five single-page plates: *The Clown* and *Toboggan*, known to be the first completed; *Monsieur Loyal* (plate III, inspired by Joseph-Léopold Loyal, ringmaster of the Cirque de l'Imperatrice and Cirque Napoléon during the Second Empire); *Icarus*, and *The Sword Swallower* (plate XIII). The background of *Icarus* contains the same star motifs as the first two cut-outs and was probably completed at nearly the same time. Since the layout of the book had not been determined when Matisse began his designs it is evident that he contemplated a book format similar to that of such earlier works as *Poésies de Stéphane Mallarmé* or the just-completed *Pasiphaé-Chant de Minos*. In those books the pictorial matter appeared on single pages. It is probable that *Pierrot's Funeral* and *The Nightmare of the White Elephant*, also completed by June 1943, were among the first ideas for double-page spreads although they both contain the undulating leaf-shape motifs that characterize some of the later compositions. Five plates, *The Codomas* (plate XI, trapeze performers), *Horse, Rider and Clown* (plate V), and the three entitled *Lagoon* share this format. The third approach to the format of the plates was undoubtedly begun with *The Circus* plate which has a definite division in the center. While this work may have been planned for the cover, it is evident that the other seven plates in this format were not. There are two schemes on which Matisse devised these cut-outs: *The Heart* (plate VII), *Forms*, and *Destiny* are composed of two panels, generally equally balanced; *The Wolf* (plate VI), *The Swimmer in the Tank* (plate XII), *The Cowboy* (plate XIV), and *The Knife Thrower* (plate XV) are designed to bridge this central division in one way or another, but not by denying that the page is folded in two.

The themes of the pages appear pertinent to their format. Aside from *The Circus*, the three plates that are divided into two panels present opposing—positive and negative—forms or subjects: *The Heart*, presented like a valentine on the right-hand (or prominent) side, faces a black void; *Forms* creates a sublime balance out of positive and negative spaces; *Destiny* places an abstract form of clinging lovers to the right opposite the black menace of a mask. Because the pictures in *Jazz* were not intended as illustrations to a text (in fact, the text that Matisse finally wrote was begun well after their completion), each contains thematic material that is often intensely subjective and open to individual interpretation. A table of contents with twenty hieroglyphs that succinctly give the emphasis of each composition was the artist's way of defining his subjects.

The sequence of the color plates has no relation to either the dates of completion or to the subject; the two earliest compositions, in fact, are placed opposite the title page and at the end of the text. The first quarter of the book contains circus subjects, followed by five compositions which have no apparent thematic link, and then five more images from the circus. However, this middle group of five is literally the heart of the book, including three images intertwined with traditional and sentimental evocations of the artistic spirit: *The Heart, Icarus,* and *Pierrot's Funeral.* In each of these plates the red form symbolizing a heart is the cynosure for the illumination of central creative dilemmas: the heart opposite the black rectangular void of inspiration; Icarus falling through the stars which he aspired to join; *Pierrot's Funeral,* the inevitable end of a life dedicated to art. In the text Matisse warns the misunderstood artist: "One creates not in hate but in love. . . love on the other hand sustains the artist." Before these three plates is placed *The Wolf* ("the better to eat you with," Matisse wittily wrote to Tériade) which, in March 1944, was easily understood as a symbol for the threatening Gestapo. The other plate in this grouping, *Forms,* manifests the artist's creative task in the simplest possible construction.

Following the second group of circus-related subjects the final five plates are introduced by *Destiny,* which Lydia Delectorskaya has described as "the small human couple (white) kneel, fearfully entwined in the face of Destiny (black and violet) menacing and dangerous." This provocative theme is followed by three colorful abstractions, *Lagoon,* Matisse's own Paradise. Finally, the volume closes with *Toboggan,* its figure tossed through space, surrounded by stars.

The complex problems of translating the saturated, glowing colors of the painted paper collages into printed sheets were already evident from the earlier attempts at reproductions in *Verve.* The first two *Verve* covers by Matisse (No. 1 and No. 8) had been printed lithographically (the cover for No. 8 in 1940 required twenty-six different inkings). Although Matisse was impressed with the care taken to reproduce his work faithfully, it must have occurred to both the artist and the publisher that the process was less than perfect. By 1943 Matisse had seen the linoleum cuts he had made for Henri de Montherlant's book *Pasiphaé—Chant de Minos* in printed form. During the Occupation most commercial presses were probably incapable of undertaking regular production. On the other hand, there were still many small shops for letterpress where text (type) and block prints (such as linoleum cuts) could be printed. Matisse was satisfied with the results obtained by the strong inking of his linoleum cuts which may explain why Tériade at first had zinc blocks made from two of the *Jazz* cut-outs (*Forms* and *The Codomas*) by Robert Ranc, director of the École Étienne. In his March 1944 letter Matisse wrote to Angèle Lamotte that all would depend upon the success of "les Bois," woodcuts probably being his understanding of the process of reproduction he thought was being used. But the photographically-made line blocks were printed with inks which simply lacked the spark of Matisse's Linel paints. Jacques Beltrand, a noted woodcut artist and printer, and a craftsman named Vaganay, printed three proofs of each of the two compositions, and one set of these in The Museum of Modern Art shows clearly the failure to capture the effect that made the cut-outs so exciting. *The Codomas,* in particular, was a parched relic, since the oranges and yellows were literally drained of their essential light.

The alternative, given the state of the printing industry after the war, was to use the traditional handicraft of stencil printing. *Pochoir*, the French word for stencil printing using a brush instead of roller or spray, had been revived in the post-World War I period with great success in reproducing the clear colors and sharply defined forms of the works of Man Ray, Sonia Delaunay, and a large group of decorative artists. The artisans of the craft still existed in Paris, but the rather uneconomical technique had fallen out of favor when color lithography printed on efficient commercial presses gradually re-emerged. Because the stencils were cut by hand and certain details in the compositions were difficult to reproduce, complex images like *The Codomas* show that there were some deviations from the cut-out composition. (For example, while Beltrand's block printing reproduces the cut-out shapes exactly, there is even a square missing in the pochoir.) Matisse was once thought to have made changes in the pochoirs, but it is hardly likely that the differences between the cut-out and the pochoir in this instance were determined by the artist. (In *The Codomas* pochoir the central lobe of the form in the upper left is lacking; the corners of two of the squares are cut off at the border.) This may well have been done by Edmond Vairel who made the stencils and printed the plates, probably after July 1946 when several of the cut-outs were signed and dated by Matisse.

From the beginning of the project the text for *Jazz* had been left in Tériade's hands. Since most of Matisse's previous work for Tériade had been for his magazines it is probable that Tériade had certain writings in mind when he asked Matisse for a book of cut-outs. In 1944, however, Matisse did ask for paper on which "to place my Jazz," so it is probable that some plan for drawn or written pages already had been discussed. In any case, by 1946 Matisse still had not turned over the majority of the cut-outs to Tériade and no text had been completed.

In June 1946 Matisse was in Paris working with Albert Skira on his longtime project, *Florilège des Amours* by Ronsard. Undoubtedly, it was during this summer-long sojourn that the idea of explaining something of his work on *Jazz* and creating "intervals of a different character" between the plates led to the manuscript text. During the summer his work on the two *Oceania* wall-hangings commissioned by Zika Ascher of London may have occasioned two passages in the text: "A simple trip from Paris to London on an airplane gives us a vision of the world that our imagination could not have revealed otherwise" and "Lagoons. Aren't you one of the seven wonders of the Paradise of painters?" The *Lagoon* cut-outs, completed nearly two years earlier, were evocations of Matisse's visit to Tahiti in 1930. Unlike other passages in the text which are "a kind of sonorous ground" to the plates, this reference to the lagoons (which he recalled in a text also written in 1946 for the *Oceania* panels "with enchantment") is entirely topical.

The idea to present the text in the artist's handwriting may have arisen from several sources. In the 1930s Picasso and the poet Paul Eluard collaborated on several prints in which poetry was handwritten on the same plate that Picasso embellished. Matisse incorporated script in his first drawings for *Poèmes de Charles d'Orléans* in 1943. Certainly, his concept of translating that 15th-century text into modern form had been inspired by the medieval illuminated manuscript, the epitome of text enhanced by decoration. In representing Charles's poetry, however, Matisse also attempted to imitate the manuscript style of the older period. In another instance, a preparatory crayon drawing for *Florilège des Amours* depicts a flower pot with the words "J'aime Marie." This composition was redrawn several times, later appearing in 1948 as an added suite to the first copies of the book. Finally, for *Lettres de la religieuse portugaise*, published in 1946 before either of the aforementioned volumes went to press, Matisse devised capitals in script to begin each paragraph.

Matisse was familiar with the notable antecedents of the form and fully conscious of his ambitions for the appearance of each book he did. Nowhere, however, did the decision to use script have more visual importance than in *Jazz*, for the lines of writing as well as the decorative arabesques, numerals, and notations to the plates have a particular distinction of achieving a perfection of compositional balance on each page. More than a means to convey verbal information, the text of *Jazz* is drawing with ink in tandem with Matisse's invention of "drawing with scissors."

The handwritten lines are formal drawings in black on undiluted white that create a rhythmic procession through the book, punctuated at precise moments with the exciting clash of the color plates. This syncopated composition is clearly what Matisse felt was the visual counterpart of jazz music. After its publication the artist was reported to have commented, "*Jazz* is rhythm and meaning."

What more is there to this virtuoso accomplishment? With *Jazz* you hold an artist's spirit in your hands. Each page reveals deeply felt ideas, years of dedication to art and its craft, innate sensitivity to visual stimuli and their perfect organization for the most exhilarating, most satisfying result. Few artists have added to their pictorial work words that have been equally important in form and meaning. The precise equilibrium of these elements in *Jazz* is Matisse's unique achievement. The dark rhythms, roiling counterpoint, happy staccatos, and jolting dissonances of this *Jazz* will sound forever. Matisse has taught the eye to hear.

Riva Castleman

The following texts have been invaluable reference sources for this essay:

Barr, Alfred H. Jr. *Matisse: His Art and His Public*. New York: The Museum of Modern Art, 1951.

Flam, Jack D., ed. *Matisse on Art*. London: Phaidon, 1973.

Flam, Jack D. "*Jazz*" and annotated catalogue in Cowart, Jack, et al., *Henri Matisse: Paper Cut-Outs*. St. Louis and Detroit: The St. Louis Art Museum and The Detroit Institute of Arts, 1977.

Fourcade, Dominique, ed. *Henri Matisse: Écrits et propos sur l'art*. Paris: Hermann, 1972.

Hommage à Tériade. Exhibition Catalogue. Paris: Centre National d'Art Contemporain, 16 May–3 September 1973.

JAZZ: THE TEXT

NOTES. After having written "he who wants to devote himself to painting must begin by cutting out his tongue," why do I feel the need to use other media than my usual ones? This time I'd like to introduce my color prints under the most favorable of conditions. For this reason I must separate them by intervals of a different character. I decided that handwriting was best suited for this purpose. The exceptional size of the writing seems necessary to me in order to be in a decorative relationship with the character of the color prints. These pages, therefore, will serve only to accompany my colors, just as asters help in the composition of a bouquet of more important flowers. *Thus, their role is purely visual.*

What can I write? I cannot very well fill these pages with the fables of La Fontaine, as I used to do as a law clerk when writing "engrossed decisions" which no one reads, not even the judge, and which are only made to use up a certain amount of official paper in accordance with the importance of the trial. All that I really have to recount are observations and notes made during the course of my life as a painter. I ask of those who will have the patience to read these notes the indulgence usually granted to the writings of painters.

THE BOUQUET. During a walk in the garden I pick flower after flower and amass them in the crook of my arm, gathering them randomly one after another. I return to the house with the idea of painting these flowers. After having arranged them in my own way, what a deception: all of their charm was lost in the arranging. What could have happened? The unconscious arrangement made during the picking, through the pleasure that prompted me to move from one flower to the next, was replaced by a willful arrangement derived from reminiscences of long-dead bouquets that left in my memory a charm of yesterday with which I now burdened the new bouquet.

Renoir once said to me: "When I have arranged a bouquet for the purpose of painting it, I always turn to the side I did not plan."

THE AIRPLANE. A simple trip from Paris to London on an airplane gives us a vision of the world that our imagination could not have revealed otherwise. Even as we are delighted by our new situation in this enchanting milieu, we are confused with memories of the cares and worries that troubled us on the earth which we glimpse far below us through the holes in the plain of clouds we ride above. And, once we return to our modest existence as pedestrians, we will no longer feel the weight of the gray sky bearing down on us, for we will remember that behind this easily penetrable wall there exist the splendor of the sun as well as a perception of unlimited space in which for a moment we felt ourselves to be so free.

Ought not one to encourage young people who have just finished their studies to take a long trip on an airplane.

THE CHARACTER OF A FACE that has been drawn does not depend on its various proportions but rather on the spiritual light that it reflects. In this way two drawings of the same face can portray the same character, even though the proportions of the faces in the two drawings may differ.

No two leaves on a fig tree are the same; each has its own form. Nonetheless, each one cries: Fig tree.

IF I HAVE CONFIDENCE IN MY HAND which draws, it is because when I was training it to serve me I resolved never to let it overshadow my feelings. When my hand is paraphrasing my feelings, I am very aware if there is any disagreement between the two of us: between my hand and that undefinable part of me that seems subjugated to it.

The hand is but an extension of sensitivity and intelligence. The more it is supple, the more it is obedient. Never should the servant girl become the mistress.

DRAWING WITH SCISSORS. To cut to the quick in color reminds me of the direct cutting of sculptors.

This book was conceived in the same spirit.

MY CURVES ARE NOT MAD. In determining the vertical direction, the plumb line along with its opposite, the horizontal, forms the compass of the draftsman. Ingres used plumb lines; in his studies of standing figures note the unerased line that passes through the sternum and the internal anklebone of the "leg that bears the weight."

Around this fictive line "the arabesque" evolves. I have derived a constant benefit from my use of the plumb line. The vertical is in my spirit. It helps me to define precisely the direction of lines, and in quick sketches I never indicate a curve, that of a branch in a landscape for example, without being aware of its relationship to the vertical.

My curves are not mad.

A NEW PAINTING should be a unique thing, a birth bringing a new face into the representation of the world through the human spirit. The artist should call forth all of his energy, his sincerity, and the greatest possible modesty in order to push aside during his work the old clichés that come so readily to his hand and can suffocate the small flower which itself never turns out as one expected.

A MUSICIAN ONCE SAID: In art, truth and reality begin when one no longer understands what one is doing or what one knows, and when there remains an energy that is all the stronger for being constrained, controlled, and compressed. It is therefore necessary to present oneself with the greatest humility: white, pure, and candid with a mind as if empty, in a spiritual state analogous to that of a communicant approaching the Lord's Table. Obviously it is necessary to have all of one's experience behind one, but to preserve the freshness of one's instincts.

DO I BELIEVE IN GOD? Yes, when I am working. When I am submissive and modest, I feel myself to be greatly helped by someone who causes me to do things which exceed my capabilities. However, I cannot acknowledge *him* because it is as if I were to find myself before a conjurer whose sleight of hand eludes me. Therefore I feel robbed of the benefits of the experience that should have been the reward for my efforts. I am ungrateful and without remorse.

YOUNG PAINTERS, PAINTERS MISUNDERSTOOD OR UNDERSTOOD TOO LATE, BEAR NO HATE. Hate is an all-devouring parasite. One creates not in hate but in love. Competition is necessary but hate . . . love on the other hand sustains the artist.

"Love is a great thing, altogether great, and it alone lightens what is heavy and endures the unjust with a just spirit, for it bears weight without considering it a burden, and makes that which is bitter sweet and savory."

"Love wants to be lofty and to be restrained by nothing lowly."

"Nothing is sweeter than love, nothing stronger, nothing loftier, nothing grander, nothing pleasanter, nothing fuller, nothing better in heaven or on earth, because love is born in God, and can only rest in God, above all creatures. He who loves soars, runs and rejoices; he is free and without bonds." *(Imitation of Christ)*

HAPPINESS. Derive happiness in oneself from a good day's work, from illuminating the fog that surrounds us. Think that all of those who have *succeeded,* when they remember the difficulties of their beginnings, cry with conviction: *"Those were the good days."* Because for most people: success = prison, and an artist should never be a *prisoner*. Prisoner? An artist should never be: prisoner of himself, prisoner of a style, prisoner of a reputation, prisoner of success, etc. Did not the Goncourts write that the artists of the great age of Japanese art changed names many times during their careers? I like that: they wanted to safeguard their freedom.

LAGOONS. Aren't you one of the seven wonders of the Paradise of painters?

HAPPY ARE THOSE WHO SING with all their heart, from the bottoms of their hearts.
    To find joy in the sky, the trees, the flowers. There are always flowers for those who want to see them.

THE AFTERLIFE. Would it not be consoling and satisfying if all those who devoted their lives to the development of their natural talents, for the benefit of all, found bliss after their deaths in a life of satisfaction in accordance with their dreams. While those who lived strictly as egoists . . .

JAZZ. These images, with their lively and violent tones, derive from crystallizations of memories of circuses, folktales, and voyages. I've written these pages to mollify the simultaneous effects of my chromatic and rhythmic improvisations; pages forming a kind of "sonorous ground" that supports them, enfolds them, and protects them, in their particularities.
    I give homage here to Angèle Lamotte and to Tériade for their perseverance and for their support for me during the realization of this book.

Translated from the French by Sophie Hawkes

Jazz

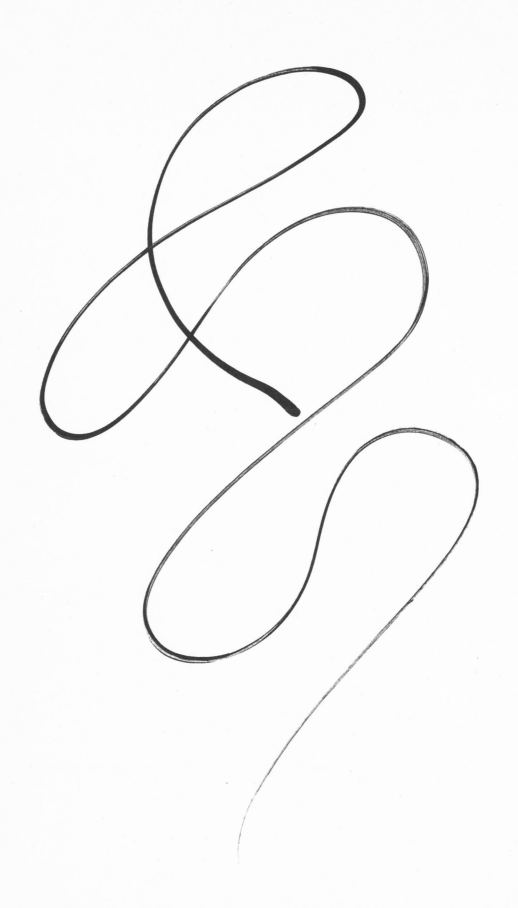

Henri Matisse

Jazz

Notes

—

Pourquoi après
avoir écrit:
" qui veut se
donner à la
peinture doit
commencer
par se faire

9

couper la
langue)", ai-je besoin
d'employer
d'autres moy-
ens que ceux
qui me sont
propres ?.
Cette fois
j'ai à présen-
ter

des planches
de couleur
dans des con-
ditions qui
leur soient
les plus favo-
rables. Pour
cela, je dois
les séparer

11

par des in-
tervalles d'un
caractère dif-
férent. J'ai
jugé que
l'écriture ma-
nuscrite con-
venait le mieux
à cet usage.
La dimension

12

exceptionnelle
de l'écriture
me semble
obligatoire
pour être en
rapport déco-
ratif avec le
caractère des
planches de
couleur .

17

Ces pages ne
servent donc
que d'accompa-
gnement à
mes couleurs,
comme des
asters aident
dans la compo-
sition d'un
bouquet de

18

fleurs d'une plus grande importance.

LEUR RÔLE EST DONC PUREMENT SPECTA-CULAIRE.

que puis-je écrire ? Je ne puis pourtant pas remplir ces pages avec

des fables de
La Fontaine,
comme je le
faisais, lorsque
j'étais clerc à
voué, pour les
"conclusions
grossoyées",
que personne
ne eût jamais,

22

même pas le
juge, et qui
ne se font que
pour user une
quantité de
papier timbré
en rapport avec
l'importance
du procès.
Il ne me reste
donc qu'à rap-
-porter

23

des remarques,
des notes prise,
au cours de
mon existence
de peintre .
Je demande
pour elles, à
ceux qui au-
ront la patience
de les lire, l'in-
dulgence que

question ac-
corde en gé-
néral aux
écrits des pein.
tres.

29

Le Bouquet.

Dans une promenade au jardin je cueille fleur après fleur pour les masser dans le creux de mon bras l'une après l'autre au hasard

de la cueillette.
Je rentre à la
maison avec
l'idée de peindre
ces fleurs. Après
en avoir fait
un arrange-
ment à ma
façon quelle
déception :
tout leur charme

31

est perdu dans
cet arrangement.
Qu'est-ie donc
arrivé ?
L'assemblage
inconscient
fait pendant
la cueillette avec
le goût qui m'a
fait aller d'une
fleur à l'autre

est remplacé
par un arran-
gement volon-
taire sorti de
réminiscences
de bouquets
morts depuis
longtemps,
qui ont laissé
dans mon

37

Souvenir leur
charme d'alors
dont j'ai chan-
gé ce nouveau
bouquet.

Renoir m'a
dit : "Quand
j'ai arrangé
un bouquet
pour le peindre,
je m'arrête

sur le côté que
je n'avais pas
prévu. »

L'Avion

Un simple voy-
age de Paris
à Londres en
avion nous don-
ne une révéla-
tion du monde
que notre ima-
gination ne
pouvait nous
faire pressentir

40

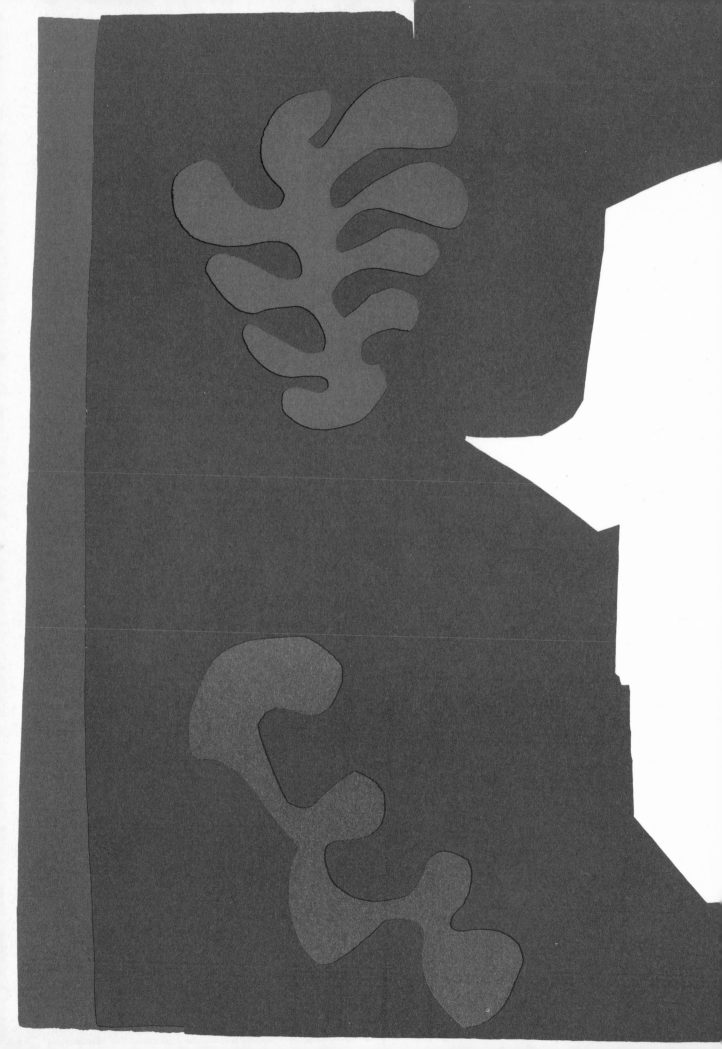

En même temps
que le senti-
ment de notre
nouvelle si-
tuation nous
ravit, il
nous rend
confus par
le souvenir
de soucis et

d'ennuis par
lesquels nous
nous sommes
laissés troubler,
sur cette terre que
nous aperce -
vons au dessous
de nous, à tra-
vers les trous de
la plaine de

46

nuages que
nous dominons
pendant qu'il
existait un
milieu enchan-
teur dans le-
quel nous
sommes. Et
lorsque nous
serons revenus

à notre mode.
.le condition
de piéton,
nous ne sen.
tirons plus
le poids du ciel
gris peser sur
nous, car nous
nous souvien.
drons que derrière

ce mur fa-
cile à traver-
ser, il existe
la splendeur
du soleil ainsi
que ta percep-
tion de l'espace
illimité dans
lequel nous nous
sommes sentis

53

un moment
si libres.

Ne devrait-on
pas faire ac-
complir un
grand voyage
en avion aux
jeunes gens
ayant terminé
leurs études.

_Le caractère
d'un visage_

dessiné ne dé-
pend pas de
ses diverses
proportions
mais d'une
lumière spi-
rituelle qu'il
reflète. Si bien
que deux

dessins du
même visage
peuvent repré-
senter le même
caractère bien
que les propor-
tions des vi-
sages de ces
deux dessins
soient différentes

58

Dans un figuier au-
cune feuille n'est pareille
à une autre ; elles sont toutes,
différentes de forme : cependant
chacune crie : Figuier.

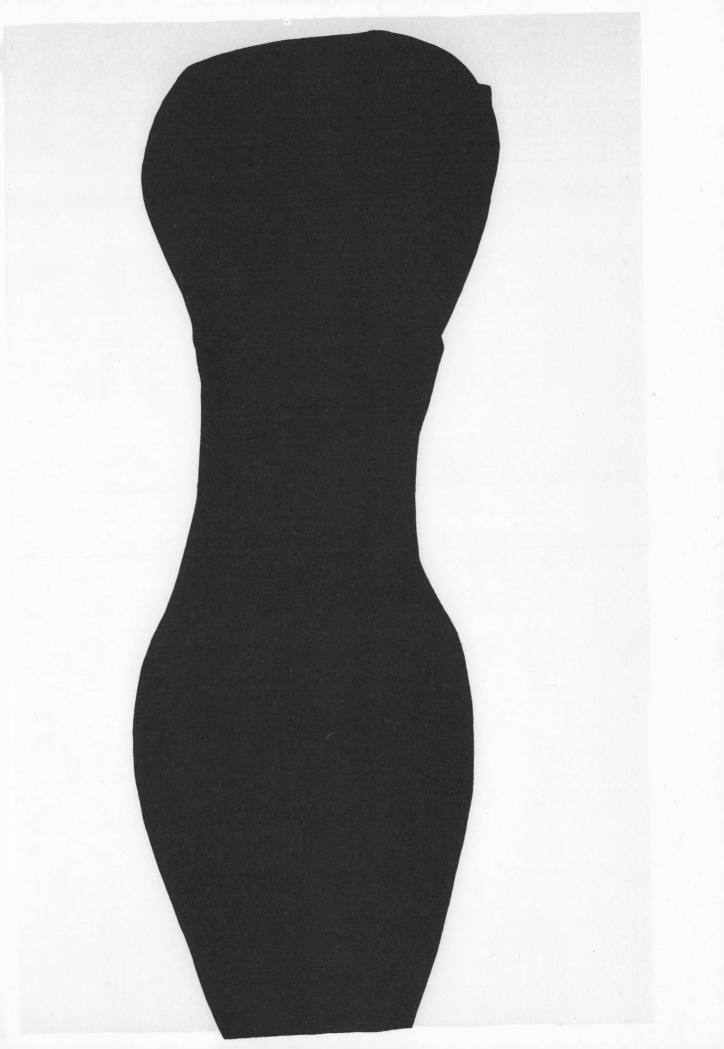

Si j'ai confiance
en ma main
qui dessine ,
c'est que pendant
que je l'habituais
à me servir ,
je me suis ef-
forcé à ne j'a-
mais lui
laisser prendre

le pas sur mon
sentiment.
Je sens très
bien, lorsqu'elle
paraphrase.
S'il y a dés-
accord entre
nous deux:
entre elle et
le je ne sais

quoi en moi
qui paraît
lui être sou-
mis.
La main n'est
que le prolonge-
ment de la
sensibilité
et de l'intel-
ligence .

Plus elle est
souple, plus
elle est-obéis-
sante. Je
ne faut pas
que la servante
devienne maî-
tresse.

Dessiner
avec des
ciseaux

—

Découper à
vif dans la
couleur me
rappelle la taille
directe des

sculpteurs.

Ce livre
a été conçu
dans cet
esprit. -

Mes courtes
ne sont pas
folles

Le fil à plomb
en détermi-
nant la direction
verticale forme
avec son opposée,
on
l'horiztale,

75

La Boussole
du dessinateur.
Ingres se
servait du
fil à plomb.
Voyez dans
ses dessins
d'études de
figures debout

cette ligne
non effacée
qui passe par
le sternum
et la malléole
interne de
" la jambe qui
porte ".
autour de cette
ligne fictive
évolue "l'arabesque".

J'ai tiré de l'usage que j'ai fait du fil à plomb un bénéfice constant. La verticale est dans mon esprit. Elle m'aide à préciser la direction

des lignes, et dans mes
dessins rapides, je n'in-
dique pas une
courbe, par
exemple celle
d'une branche
dans un pay-
sage, sans avoir

conscience de
son rapport
avec la verti-
cale.

mes courbes
ne sont pas
folles.

Un nouveau

tableau doit être une chose unique, une naissance ap. portant une figure nouvelle dans la représen. tation du mon. de à travers

l'esprit humain.
L'artiste doit
apporter toute
son énergie,
sa sincérité
et la modestie
la plus grande
pour écarter
pendant son
travail les
vieux clichés

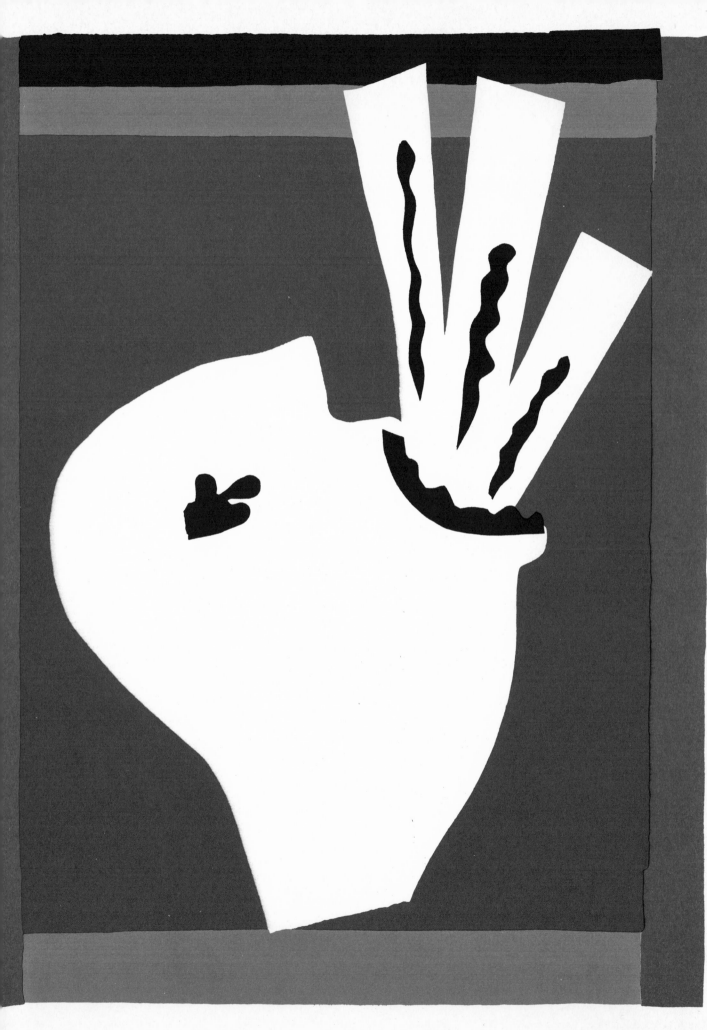

qui viennent
si facilement
à sa main
et peuvent
étouffer la petite fleur
qui ne vient,
elle, jamais
telle qu'on l'at-
tend .

Un musicien

a dit :

En art (la vérité,
le réel commence
quand on ne com-
prend plus rien
à ce qu'on fait-,
à ce qu'on sait,
et qu'il reste
en vous une

94

énergie d'autant
plus forte qu'elle
est contrariée,
compressée,
comprimée.
Il faut alors
se présenter
avec la plus
grande humi-
lité, tout-blanc,
tout-pur, candide,

le cerveau sem-
blant vide, dans
un état d'esprit
analogue à celui
du communiant
approchant la
Sainte Table .
Il faut évidemment
avoir tout acquit^{son}
derrière soi et
avoir su garder

la fraîcheur
de l'Instinct.

Si je crois en Dieu ?

Oui, quand je travaille. Quand je suis soumis & modeste, je me sens tellement aidé par quelqu'un qui me

102

fait faire des
choses qui me
surpassent.
Pourtant je
ne me sens
envers <u>lui</u>'aucune
reconnaissance
car c'est comme
si je me trouvais
devant un pres-
tidigitateur

dont je ne puis
percer les tours.
Je me trouve
alors frustré
du bénéfice
de l'expérience
qui devait être
la récompense
de mon effort.
Je suis ingrat-
sans remords.

Jeunes peintres,
peintres incom-
pris ou tardive-
ment compris
pas de Haine

La haine est
un parasite
qui dévore tout.
" on ne construit

109

pas dans la
haine mais
dans l'amour.
L'émulation
est nécessaire,
mais la
haine ...
L'amour au
contraire soi.
tient l'artiste.

110

« C'est une grande
« chose que
« l'amour, un
« bien tout à
« fait grand,
« qui seul rend
« léger ce qui
« est pesant
« et endure d'une
« âme égale ce
« qui est inégal.

« Car il porte
« le poids sans
« qu'il soit un
« fardeau et rend
« doux et savoure
« tout ce qui est
« amer ...
« L'amour veut
« être en haut
« et n'être retenu
« par rien de
« bas ...

Rien n'est plus doux que l'amour, rien n'est plus fort, rien n'est plus haut, rien n'est plus large, rien de plus aimable, rien de plus plein, rien de meilleur

137

« au ciel & sur
« la terre, par
« ce que l'amou
« est né de Dieu
« et ne peut-se
« reposer sinon
« en Dieu, au
« dessus de toutes
« les créatures.
« Celui qui aime
« vole, court et

118

« se réjouit ;
« il est libre et
« rien ne le re-
« tient ».   (Im. de J.C.)

⌒

Bonheur .

Tirer le bonheur
de soi-même,
d'une bonne
journée de
travail, de

l'éclaircie
qu'elle a pu
apporter dans
le brouillard
qui nous en-
toure. Penser
que tous ceux
qui sont arrivés,
en se souvenant
des difficultés de
leurs débuts,

J'écrient ~~avec~~
avec conviction:
"C'était le bon
temps". Car
pour la plupart:
arrivée = Prison,
et l'artiste ne
doit jamais être
prisonnier.
Prisonnier?
un artiste ne

doit jamais
être : ~~prisonnier~~
prisonnier de
lui-même, pri-
sonnier d'une
manière, pri-
sonnier d'une
réputation,
prisonnier d'un
succès, etc...
Les Goncourt

n'ont-ils pas
écrit que les
artistes japo-
-nais de la grande
époque changèaient
de nom plus i'un
fois dans leur vie.
J'aime ça : ils
voulaient sauve-
garder leurs
libertés ~

Lagons,

ne seriez-vous pas une des sept merveilles du Paradis des peintres?

ℰℬ

Heureux ceux
qui chantent
de tout leur coeur,
dans la droiture
de leur coeur.

Trouver la Joie
dans le ciel,
dans les arbres,
dans les fleurs.

133

Il y a des fleurs
partout pour
qui veut bien
les voir.

134

La vie future.

ne serait-il pas
consolant, sa-
tisfaisant que
tous ceux qui
ont donné leur
vie au dévelop-
pement de leurs
dons naturels,
au profit de
tous, jouissent

après leur mort,
d'une vie de sa-
tisfactions en
accord avec leur
désir. Tandis
que ceux qui
ont vécu en
étroits égoïstes...

Jazz
—

Ces images
aux timbres
vifs & violents,
sont venues
de cristal-
lisations
de souvenirs
du cirque,

de contes
populaires
ou de voyage.
J'ai fait ces
pages d'écri-
tures pour
apaiser les
réactions,
simultanées

de mes im-
provisations
chromatiques
et rythmées,
pages formant
comme un
"fond sonore"
qui les porte,
les entouré
et protège

ainsi leurs
particularités
—
Je rends ici
hommage à
angèle Lamotte
et à Tériade,
leur persévé-
-rance m'a
soutenu dans
la réalisation de
ce livre.

Table des Images

CET OUVRAGE A ÉTÉ ACHEVÉ D'IMPRIMER, PAR LES SOINS DE TÉRIADE POUR LES ÉDITIONS VERVE, LE 30 SEPTEMBRE 1947. LES PLANCHES ONT ÉTÉ EXÉCUTÉES AU POCHOIR D'APRÈS LES COLLAGES ET SUR LES DÉCOUPAGES DE HENRI MATISSE, PAR EDMOND VAIREL QUI A UTILISÉ LES MÊMES GOUACHES DE LINEL QUE L'ARTISTE. LA COUVERTURE ET LES PAGES DU MANUSCRIT ONT ÉTÉ GRAVÉES ET IMPRIMÉES PAR DRAEGER FRÈRES. IL A ÉTÉ TIRÉ SUR VÉLIN D'ARCHES DEUX CENT CINQUANTE EXEMPLAIRES NUMÉROTÉS DE 1 A 250 ET VINGT EXEMPLAIRES HORS COMMERCE NUMÉROTÉS DE I A XX. TOUS LES EXEMPLAIRES ONT ÉTÉ SIGNÉS PAR L'ARTISTE. IL A ÉTÉ TIRÉ EN OUTRE CENT ALBUMS COMPORTANT EXCLUSIVEMENT TOUTES LES PLANCHES DU LIVRE.

EXEMPLAIRE NUMÉRO 43

H matisse

Facsimile of the colophon to the original edition of 250 copies, signed by the artist and published by Tériade for Éditions Verve on 30 September 1947.